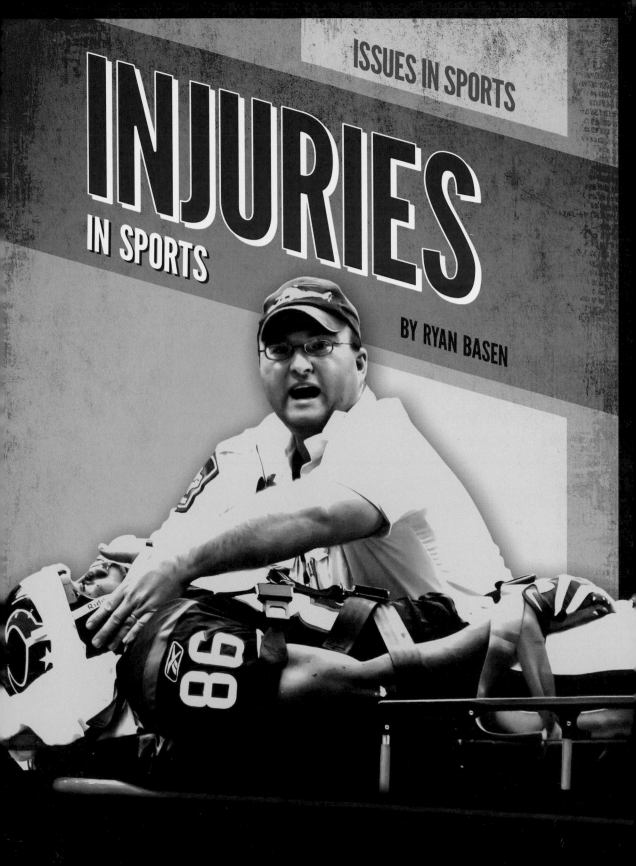

INJURIES

IN SPORTS

BY RYAN BASEN

Published by ABDO Publishing Company, PO Box 398166, Minneapolis, MN 55439. Copyright © 2014 by Abdo Consulting Group, Inc. International copyrights reserved in all countries. No part of this book may be reproduced in any form without written permission from the publisher. SportsZone™ is a trademark and logo of ABDO Publishing Company.

Printed in the United States of America,
North Mankato, Minnesota
102013
012014

Editor: Chrös McDougall
Series Designer: Craig Hinton

Photo credits: Tony Gutierrez/AP Images, cover, 1; Richard Lipski/AP Images, 5; Gerry Broome/AP Images, 7; Matt Slocum/AP Images, 10; Luis M. Alvarez/AP Images, 13; Marcio Jose Sanchez/AP Images, 15; Elise Amendola/AP Images, 17; Armando Franca/AP Images, 20; Athlon Sports/AP Images, 23; Morry Gash/AP Images, 28; Bill Kostroun/AP Images, 31; The Star Tribune, Carlos Gonzalez/AP Images, 33, 39; Minnesota Public Radio, Jeffrey Thompson/AP Images, 36; Evan Vucci/AP Images, 41; Mari Darr-Welch/AP Images, 43; The Daily Reflector, Greg Eans/AP Images, 47; Jae C. Hong/AP Images, 49; Andy King/AP Images, 51; Charles Rex Arbogast/AP Images, 54; David Zalubowski/AP Images, 59

Library of Congress Control Number: 2013946565

Cataloging-in-Publication Data

Basen, Ryan.
 Injuries in sports / Ryan Basen.
   p. cm. -- (Issues in sports)
Includes bibliographical references and index.
ISBN 978-1-62403-123-6
1. Sports injuries--Juvenile literature. 2. Athletic injuries--Juvenile literature.   I. Title.
617.1--dc23

                                                2013946565

Content Consultant: Alex B. Diamond, D.O., M.P.H.
Assistant Professor of Orthopaedics and Rehabilitation
Assistant Professor of Pediatrics
Medical Director, Program for Injury Prevention in Youth Sports (PIPYS)
Vanderbilt University Medical Center
Team Physician - Vanderbilt University, Nashville Predators, Nashville Sounds
Vanderbilt Sports Medicine

TABLE OF CONTENTS

PAIN IN THE GAME

Robert Griffin III was in pain. The Washington Redskins' star quarterback felt a searing pain in his right knee. More than 84,000 nervous Redskins fans watched quietly as the 6-foot-2 (188-cm), 216-pound (98-kg) Griffin lay on the grass at FedEx Field.

It was January 2013—Griffin's rookie season in the National Football League (NFL). Yet this was the second time in one month that the 22-year-old had injured the knee. Suddenly one of the league's bright young stars had an uncertain future.

Griffin was taken out of the game. Doctors later determined that the player had torn two ligaments in his knee. Griffin faced reconstructive

surgery. His recovery after that was impossible to predict. He would for sure be out for several months. But even Griffin's surgeon could not predict when Griffin would be able to play again. Griffin had thrived in the NFL as a quarterback who could both pass and run with the ball. Only time would tell if he could ever fully regain his speed and footwork.

Doctors, fans, analysts, and journalists all weighed in about Griffin's injury. So did his teammates, coaches, and even Griffin himself. One topic they debated was whether Griffin should have been on the field in the first place. After all, he had injured the same knee just weeks earlier.

Injuries in sports, however, can be complicated. Athletes are often nicked up or playing through nagging injuries during a season. This is especially true in a physical sport like football. So teams and athletes have to assess the risks of the situation.

One factor is that most athletes are simply eager to play. They are competitive. As long as they are physically able, they want to be out on the field. That is true among athletes from the youth to the professional ranks. This approach can lead to problems, though. Sometimes playing through injuries can make the injuries worse. Or sometimes injuries are worse than they feel. Those were some of the issues Griffin and the Redskins had to consider in 2013.

The quarterback was playing hurt, but his team needed him in the playoffs. Ultimately, Griffin and the team decided to risk Griffin's health and go for the win. Their decision might have affected his entire career.

An athletic trainer treats Duke University ▲ basketball player Chelsea Gray's knee during a rehabilitation session.

INJURIES ON ALL LEVELS

Injuries are simply a part of sports. Athletes, coaches, and league officials make efforts to minimize the risks. But when taking part in physical activity, the risk of injury is always there.

Athletes can be injured in many ways. Football and hockey players crash into each other at high speeds. That puts their bodies and brains at risk on every play. But even a long-distance runner can develop an injury without ever contacting another athlete. The runner might get a stress fracture from overuse or pull a muscle.

Young athletes have an increased risk of injury. There are many reasons for this. They are going through a lot of change and development in their bodies. This affects strength, flexibility, endurance, balance, and other areas. Skeletal immaturity is another factor. This means that kids are more likely to break bones as opposed to straining muscles. In addition, youth athletes are often exposed to a great deal of physical activity in sports. This leads to more opportunities to get injured.

Some experts believe that young kids should avoid collision sports until around age 14. Collision sports are those such as football and ice hockey where colliding is part of the play. Studies have found that most bodies are mature enough to handle checking at age 14. Until then, the experts argue, players should not check in hockey. Doctors are researching and debating whether or not similar rules should apply to tackling in youth football.

Another issue is the long-term consequences of sports injuries. For example, prior injury to a joint is the leading cause of arthritis.

Athletes might be able to play through a nagging injury during their teens or twenties. However, those nagging injuries sometimes develop into a lifetime limp or even worse. Patients can have issues of pain, mobility, and function. This can lead to mental and emotional problems.

Experts have also noticed that the number of injured athletes is on the rise. Elite and even youth athletes are dedicating more time toward training than ever before. Often they specialize in one sport. This puts athletes at higher risk of overuse injuries. And athletes today are getting bigger, faster, and stronger. That is not always safe. In collision sports, it means that athletes are more able to hurt each other. These trends are likely to continue. However, sports medicine and sports leagues are constantly working to counter that trend.

Still, as long as athletes are training and competing, there will be injuries. And as long as there are injuries, there will be people working to limit the risk and improve the recovery process.

GRIFFIN'S INJURY WOES

Griffin had dealt with knee injuries in college. More knee issues began to develop in December 2012. He sprained a ligament in his right knee during a game against the Baltimore Ravens. Griffin sat out for one game. Then he came back to lead the Redskins in their final two games. However, he did so wearing a bulky, black knee brace. It showed that his knee had not fully recovered from the sprain.

Griffin was determined to play, however. And he led his team to two more victories and a division title. He wore the knee brace

RISKS ALL AROUND

Athletes suffer injuries from crashing into each other in sports such as football and hockey. However, researchers have found that youth and high school athletes are just as likely to be injured in collision sports as they are in contact sports. Contact sports are sports where contact is inadvertently made during play. In high school, players in contact sports such as volleyball, soccer, and basketball have high rates of ankle injuries, for example. Another study notes that overtraining increases injury risk. This comes from working out too often or too hard. In addition, competing often against bigger, older, more physically mature opponents also increases injury likelihood among young athletes. Risk of injury usually increases as the level of competition rises as well.

throughout the run. But the Redskins were winning and Griffin had not suffered any setbacks. Because of this, few questioned the decision to let him play.

Then came the January 6, 2013, playoff game against the Seattle Seahawks. Griffin started off fast. He tossed two touchdown passes in the first quarter. The Redskins led the visiting Seahawks 14–0.

During Washington's second drive, however, Griffin had thrown across his body. He was scrambling to his right. But he planted his right leg awkwardly to make a throw to his left. Griffin limped back to the huddle. Then he threw his second touchdown pass two plays later as if nothing was bothering him.

A Seattle defender hit Griffin late after that pass, though. Griffin usually raced back to the huddle after plays with a sprinter's speed. After this hit, he limped back to join his teammates. He slowed down on the field, too. Seattle scored three consecutive touchdowns to take a 21–14 lead in the fourth quarter.

Just more than six minutes remained in the game. The Redskins faced a second-and-long in their own territory. Griffin attempted to snare a low shotgun snap. He reached down for the ball and planted his leg in the muddy field. Then his knee gave out. Griffin crumpled to the field.

The stadium fell silent for a few moments. Griffin's teammates kneeled around him and bowed their heads. Then, as trainers attended to Griffin after the play, chants of his nickname "R-G-3" echoed throughout the crowd. Griffin eventually rose to his feet and walked to the Redskins' sideline. He did not return to the game.

SECOND-GUESSING

After Griffin went down against Seattle, observers were quick to offer their opinions. They wondered why Griffin had rushed back to the lineup after the initial injury against Baltimore. They questioned if he should have allowed more time for the sprain to heal properly. Others pointed out that if Griffin was healthy enough to play through the sprain, he was right to be out there playing.

The Seattle game brought its own set of circumstances. Griffin had hurt the knee again in the first quarter. Some observers wondered why he didn't take himself out of the game then. He had stayed in the game when he was clearly hobbling. In fact, he insisted on staying in. But some people argued that the coaches should have overruled Griffin.

There was no consensus on what should have happened. However, both Griffin and Redskins coach Mike Shanahan defended the decision to keep Griffin in the game.

STILL IN PAIN

The *Washington Post* conducted a survey of more than 500 retired NFL players in 2013. In it, 9 of 10 players reported they suffered aches or pains every day. Eighty-three percent said they had undergone orthopedic surgeries. Those are procedures performed on hips, knees, ankles, and shoulders. This study was consistent with a 2009 University of Michigan survey. The Michigan survey found that 8 of 10 former NFL players dealt with pain daily. However, 9 in 10 players surveyed by *The Post* said they were glad they played NFL football despite the long-term pain.

"I thought he did enough for us this year to have that opportunity to stay in the football game," Shanahan said. "He said: 'Hey, trust me. I want to be in there, and I deserve to be in there.' And I couldn't disagree with him."

Griffin explained himself with a sense of pride. "I'm the best option for this team," he said. "That's why I'm the starter."

Explanations such as these are common in sports. Athletes view themselves as the ultimate competitors. They value traits such as trust, toughness, being a good teammate,

and personal integrity. Critics and fans praise players for fighting through
pain and coming through for their teams. But as more and more is learned
about sports injuries and their long-term effects, the belief in these traits
is increasingly being questioned.

CHAPTER 2

Green Bay Packers wide receiver Jordy Nelson hauls in a touchdown pass during Super Bowl XLV in February 2011. ▶

INJURY WAVE

It was a Sunday night in early February 2011. The Green Bay Packers had just defeated the Pittsburgh Steelers 31–25 to win Super Bowl XLV. Packers tailback James Starks rushed for 52 yards. Wide receiver Jordy Nelson caught nine passes for 140 yards and a touchdown. On defense, cornerback Pat Lee helped stop the Steelers on their final drive.

The performances by Starks, Nelson, and Lee were notable because they came in reserve roles. They stepped up when the Packers suffered an astonishing number of injuries in the regular season.

NFL teams can carry 53 players on their active rosters during the season. Those players can be replaced on the active roster if injured.

In 2010, the Packers lost 15 players to injured reserve. That meant those players suffered season-ending injuries at some point during the year. Green Bay lost 31 players to a total of 206 games due to injury that season.

These Packers represented a modern professional sports champion. A popular saying in the NFL is "next man up." That refers to backups who have to step in. Teams must have depth to win in the NFL. Backups must be prepared to enter games at any time. And with so many injuries, the backups are often called on.

Injuries have always occurred in sports, from youth to professional levels. However, the pressure on athletes has become greater over the years. For many years, athletes earned a paycheck but hardly a fortune playing sports. Many athletes even had other jobs in the offseason. And while they were in good shape, they rarely lifted weights. Athletes still got injured, but not in the alarming numbers we hear about today.

Today, there is a lot of money in professional sports. That brings more pressure to succeed. Most professional athletes train and compete as a full-time job. In addition to training more, today's athletes also have better training techniques. So today's athletes are bigger, stronger, and faster than those of just a few years ago. However, in sports such as football and hockey, that means players are hitting each other with more force than ever before. In all sports, that means increased strain on the body. As a result, injuries today come in a whole new variety and in greater numbers than ever.

Scottish tennis player Andy Murray reacts after ▲
spraining his ankle during a 2007 match.

STARTLING INJURY FIGURES

According to the *Washington Post*, the NFL reported approximately 30,000 injuries during the 10 seasons from 2002 to 2011. That figure included 4,500 injuries suffered by players in 2011. Approximately 2,000 players suit up in an NFL game every season. That means the average NFL player suffered 2.25 injuries in 2011.

Youth sports have seen injury numbers grow as well. Safe Kids Worldwide is an organization dedicated to preventing youth sports injuries around the world. It estimates that more than 38 million kids and teens play sports in the United States. And one in three youth athletes playing a team sport will miss games or practices due to injury. Safe Kids Worldwide also reported that as many as 62 percent of all youth sports injuries occur during practices.

The most common youth sports injuries are sprains and strains. Sprains occur when a ligament near a joint stretches too far or tears. A strain is the stretching or tearing of the muscle or tendon structures.

Strains are also known as pulled muscles. Catastrophic injuries are rare in youth sports. These are severe injuries to the spine, spinal cord, or brain. However, some kids do die or suffer other major injuries each year through sports. Around 775,000 kids ages 14 and under have to visit emergency rooms each year because of sports injuries. Most of these injuries are caused by collisions with other players, falls, or being struck by the ball or another object during play.

Sports generally become more serious and competitive around high school. And high school athletes suffer approximately 2 million sports injuries each year. An injury is defined as an event in which an athletic trainer evaluates a player and has enough

/////////////////////////////

OVERUSE INJURIES

Not all injuries come from contact. "Overuse" injuries are common in many sports, especially among youths. These injuries come when an athlete is too active in a given sport or activity, such as baseball or weightlifting. They are caused by overuse of the same joints and tendons without enough recovery time. This can cause injuries in developing bodies. Overuse injuries account for about half of all injuries suffered by kids and teens. According to *Sports Illustrated*, "By introducing variety, moderation, and rest into an everyday sports routine, a child's risk can be cut to nearly zero." However, if an athlete suffers overuse injuries, doctors say he or she should treat them immediately. Failure to treat these injuries can lead to more serious problems down the road.

///

evidence to restrict the player from participation. Around 30,000 high school athletes are hospitalized each year due to sports injuries as well.

BIGGER, FASTER, STRONGER ATHLETES

Athletes at the highest levels are bigger, faster, and stronger than ever. They are also suffering injuries at a higher rate than ever. This is especially true in collision sports.

Hockey is one of the most popular collision sports. The game has changed over the years as players have become bigger and stronger. Alex Ovechkin is one of the biggest stars in the National Hockey League (NHL). He is 6-foot-3 (191 cm) and 230 pounds (104 kg). He is big but not huge in today's NHL. The average NHL player in 2010 was just taller than 6-foot-1 (185 cm) and 204 pounds (93 kg). But Boston Bruins defenseman Zdeno Chara is 6-foot-9 (206 cm) and 255 pounds (116 kg). The bigger and stronger players have changed how the sport is played. The authors of a book about Ovechkin compared today's game to that of a generation ago.

"Players were smaller, shifts longer, and the pace of the game often a walk compared to the modern game's dead sprint," they wrote.

Injuries are not limited to collisions, though. Many athletes have suffered major knee or ankle injuries without ever making contact with somebody else. LaVar Arrington was a star linebacker in the NFL for seven seasons. He was playing for the New York Giants during a *Monday Night Football* game in October 2006. Suddenly he felt a pop in his lower left leg. He fell to the ground.

Soccer player Kelley O'Hara is carried off the field with an injury during a 2011 training session with the US women's national team.

Arrington assumed an opposing player must have hit him in the leg. But when he looked around, no one was there. Arrington was taken off the field in a cart. He later learned he had torn an Achilles' tendon in his lower leg. An Achilles often tears when an athlete suddenly lengthens the tendon, near the heel. The injury meant Arrington would have to miss the rest of the season. He later retired without playing again.

In a game a few weeks later, Philadelphia Eagles quarterback Donovan McNabb rolled to his right, toward the sideline. A Tennessee Titans defender lightly pushed McNabb. The play looked like many others in McNabb's career. This time, however, he immediately grabbed his leg.

INJURIES IN SPORTS

McNabb had to be carted off the field. It was soon determined that he had torn the anterior cruciate ligament (ACL) in his right knee. That injury usually requires 8 to 12 months of recovery. So the star quarterback was out for the remainder of the season. The injury wasn't intentional. In some ways it was a fluke. But it ultimately affected McNabb's career.

When he came back in 2007, he had to wear a protective knee brace. McNabb was only 30, but the injuries slowed him down. He had been an All-Pro player with the Eagles. In 2010, the Eagles promoted a younger quarterback and traded McNabb to the Washington Redskins. But McNabb was a shell of his former self. He lasted just one season in Washington. And after the Minnesota Vikings released him during the 2011 season, McNabb was without a job.

At 34, McNabb was not an old man. He felt he could still play pro football and was not ready to retire. But the 13-year veteran was fortunate. In injury-riddled pro sports today, playing that long is considered a very long career.

//

HIGHER RISK FOR GIRLS

Young female athletes are more likely than males to suffer ACL tears. It is known that girls have more muscle and nerve imbalance than boys. That imbalance is believed to be the main cause for ACL tears. There are other theories as well. Girls don't naturally grow as much muscle as boys to stabilize and support joints. They also run "in a less-flexed, more upright position" than boys, according to an article in the *New York Times*. This "may put them at greater [injury] risk when changing directions and landing from jumps." Soccer, volleyball, lacrosse, and basketball are thus more likely than other sports to cause injuries in young female athletes.

//

LONG-TERM CONSEQUENCES

D on Majkowski suddenly became a breakout star during the 1989 NFL season. The Green Bay Packers' quarterback tossed 27 touchdown passes, threw for an NFL-high 4,318 yards, and led the Packers to 10 wins. That was their most victories in 17 seasons. Many of the Packers' wins that season were dramatic. Seven games were won by four points or fewer. Green Bay fans affectionately nicknamed the third-year player "Magik Man" during that dream season.

Two decades later, Majkowski needed magic to go through a day without feeling any pain. He has undergone almost 20 surgeries on his ankle, shoulder, and back. A metal plate and 13 screws fuse together

NFL RULE CHANGES

Football is a naturally violent sport. Stories of former players suffering from injuries put a spotlight on that. So the NFL has made some rule changes in an effort to make the game safer. For example, kickoffs now take place from the 35-yard line instead of the 30-yard line. The league also fines and penalizes players for dangerous hits. These hits include shots to the head or hits against defenseless receivers. In addition, the league also put restrictions on practices. This includes limiting the number of offseason workouts a team can hold and the number of full-pad practices a team can hold during the season. All of these measures are designed to limit the number and severity of collisions players take during their careers.

his left foot with his ankle. That makes walking difficult. He has two steel plates in his back. He also is stricken by bone spurs, torn ligaments, degenerative arthritis, and stripped cartilage in his knees.

Majkowski had occasionally heard stories of former players dealing with painful retirements. But he did not pay those warnings much attention.

"You hear stories of what you will have to face when you get older," said Majkowski, who retired in 1996. "You don't put much merit in that when you're younger."

Majkowski is not alone. Hundreds of former athletes go on to suffer from physical and mental pain in their retirements. Some of the pain is left over from major injuries that never fully healed. Other pain is from years of wear and tear taking a toll on their bodies. These long-term injuries are most common in collision sports such as football and ice hockey.

Like Majkowski, many of these athletes were warned of future problems when they were active. But they continued to play through pain and undergo surgeries to extend their careers.

Elite athletes face tough decisions when they suffer injuries. Some decide to play through the pain and deal with the consequences later in life. The money, fame, enjoyment, and competition are too much for them to walk away from. On rare occasions, however, there are some athletes who retire while still in their prime.

SHORT-TERM THINKING

Many athletes do whatever they can to continue playing. There are many reasons for doing so. Some athletes are ultra competitive and cannot imagine their lives without sports. They refuse to retire until no team wants them. Others might continue competing simply to earn money to support themselves or their families.

Roman Oben was faced with the decision late in his NFL career. He decided to have two reconstructive surgeries so he could continue playing.

"I knew then at 33, 34 years old, I was going to have trouble walking when I'm older," the former offensive lineman said. "I said, 'I don't care. I deserve to work as hard as I can to improve the quality of life for my family.' "

Many pro athletes go to great lengths to play through pain and injury. They do so knowing they might be setting themselves up for pain and even deformity in the long term.

Bill Buckner took a similar risk during the 1986 baseball season. The Boston Red Sox first baseman suffered from swollen joints and muscles.

To mask the pain, he received nine cortisone shots during the season. The 36-year-old Buckner also wrapped his aching joints in athletic tape and took two anti-inflammatory pills every day. Those measures made him feel strong enough to play. However, they did nothing to address the recovery.

According to *One Pitch Away*, a famous book about the 1986 playoffs:

Buckner knew that wasn't good for him. There would be a price to pay somewhere down the line. But that was a decision he had made, and he was willing to live with it.

NHL RULE CHANGES

The NHL has also taken steps to improve safety. The league requires players to wear newer and better safety equipment. It rounded the glass near player benches. This lessens the impact should a player be hit into this space. The NHL also banned players from intentionally targeting and checking an opponent in the head. "I know people say players have to police it themselves," said Brian Campbell, an NHL defenseman. "But how that happens is through tougher suspensions and fines. It takes the league to step up." However, a 2013 study concluded that the rule changes did not affect concussion rates. It was a signal that the effort to make sports safer is ongoing.

Other ballplayers had quit the game rather than risk long-term health problems. Not Buckner. He wanted to squeeze every at-bat out of his career. He didn't want to look back 10, 20 years from now and wonder what else he might have accomplished.

Ultimately, Buckner had a good season at the plate. The injuries hurt his fielding, however. And the fielding woes were highlighted at the worst possible moment. Buckner was playing first base in Game 6 of the World Series against the New York Mets. He struggled to get low enough on a routine ground ball. It ended up rolling through his legs and into the outfield. Boston went on to lose that game and the series.

BRAIN INJURIES

In recent years, attention to brain injuries has increased tremendously. As researchers learn more about concussions and other brain injuries, sports leagues have struggled to adapt.

Concussions are traumatic brain injuries that occur when a hit or jolt causes a person's brain to shake inside the skull. The results can be anything from simply "seeing stars" to extreme headaches, loss of balance and coordination, fatigue, and memory problems. Most concussions last only a few days. Sometimes the effects last much longer.

Corey Koskie had played 988 games in Major League Baseball (MLB) going into July 5, 2006. In his 989th game, the Milwaukee Brewers' third baseman fell backward while trying to make a catch. The fall appeared to be a routine happening. But Koskie hit his head as he went down. It resulted in a concussion. He never played another game in MLB.

Koskie later estimated that he had suffered at least eight concussions before then. But the symptoms of his latest concussion would not go away. Finally, in 2009, new treatment helped Koskie begin to feel better.

Doctors have learned a lot about concussions in the years that followed Koskie's fall. Efforts have been made to make sports safer. For example, the NFL has looked into new helmets that can better protect the head. The league has also adjusted its rules to limit contact in practice

▲ The Milwaukee Brewers' Corey Koskie falls while trying to catch a foul ball against the Cincinnati Reds in 2006. The fall resulted in a concussion.

and to limit hits to the head in games. In hockey, most youth leagues now ban checking for the youngest players. Studies have found that brains are most vulnerable in young people.

Many leagues have also taken a hard line on concussion management. Research has found that a second blow to the head before a concussion has healed can cause lifelong brain damage or even death.

Athletes by nature are competitive. Many believe they can play through a headache or other concussion symptoms. But sports leagues now make the decision for the players. In the NFL, a player showing any signs of concussion must sit out for the rest of the day. The player is not allowed to return to the game even if the symptoms go away. Many other leagues have followed this example.

EARLY RETIREMENT

Tiki Barber had a career season in 2005. The New York Giants running back led the NFL with 2,390 yards from scrimmage. He remained one of the league's top rushers in 2006. And the Giants were contenders for a Super Bowl. That is when Barber announced he would retire at the end of the season.

Barber was only 31 and healthy. The Giants were among the NFL's best teams. And if Barber played, the Giants owed him $8.3 million over the next two seasons. People wondered why Barber would walk away from all of that.

Barber, however, was most concerned with preserving his body for the long term. He had two children and a wife whom he

LONG-TERM BRAIN DAMAGE

Junior Seau was a fearsome linebacker for 20 seasons in the NFL. Then one day in 2012 he committed suicide. Over his career—from youth to high school to college to the NFL—Seau had taken many hits to the head. The vast majority of them did not cause a concussion. But after he died, researchers found a disease called chronic traumatic encephalopathy (CTE) in his brain. Among its symptoms are personality changes, memory loss, and dementia. Some experts believe that head trauma from sports can cause CTE. They believe even smaller jolts like repeatedly heading a soccer ball might lead to CTE as well. No one can say for sure if CTE played a role in Seau's suicide. But hundreds of ex-NFL players have reported experiencing long-term brain damage after retiring.

Tiki Barber of the New York Giants was one of ▶
the best running backs in the NFL before his
surprising retirement in 2006.

wanted to care for. He feared mounting injuries would drain them of time, love, and money. Plus he saw other opportunities outside of playing football where he could have a successful career, such as broadcasting.

His wife "wanted him to leave football in one piece," wrote veteran NFL reporter Mark Maske in *War Without Death*, a book about the 2006 NFL season. "He shared that desire. He didn't want to be unable to walk in his early fifties."

Don Majkowski might not be able to say the same thing. Injuries forced him to retire at age 31. By his late forties, he struggled to walk. So did many of his former teammates. Majkowski attends Packers reunions, where organizers plan events such as dinners and golf outings. Many players cannot even play golf, however, because of their injuries.

Says Majkowski, "We just go and ride around on the golf carts."

CHAPTER 4

Minnesota high school hockey player Jack Jablonski is transferred to a new medical facility in January 2013. He was paralyzed during a game a few weeks earlier. ▶

INJURIES IN YOUTH COLLISION SPORTS

Jack Jablonski saw the puck in the corner of the rink. The Minnesota high school hockey player had been playing hockey for years. The play in this 2011 game began just like dozens of plays he had been a part of over the years. Jablonski skated toward the boards and prepared for a collision. Then an opponent checked him from behind as they battled for the puck.

At first, the play looked routine. Players are often checked into the boards as they fight for loose pucks. It's part of hockey.

However, what happened next to Jablonski is a much more rare part of hockey. The 16-year-old sophomore crashed into the boards. He fell

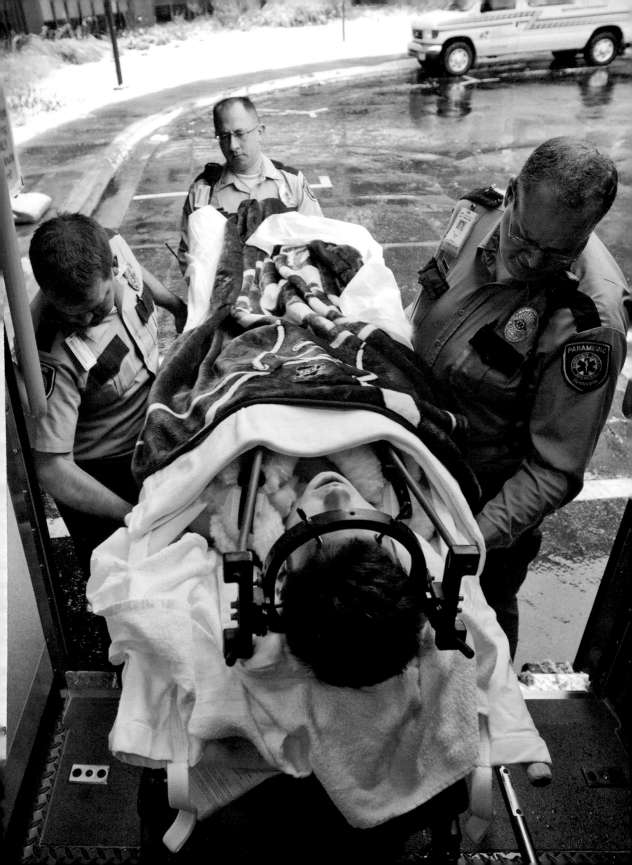

CHECKING BANS

Those in favor of checking bans have evidence to support their beliefs. A 2012 study in Canada surveyed youth hockey players. It found that players who body checked at the peewee level (ages 11-12) were three times more likely to suffer a major injury than those players who did not. The researchers recommended kids wait until age 13 to start checking. That study helped lead to Hockey Canada banning checking at the peewee level and below. However, peewee coaches were encouraged to still teach checking fundamentals in practice. The belief is that serious injuries are less likely to occur in practice because it is more controlled than a game.

to the ice and did not get up. Jablonski lay motionless. The game was stopped. Medical personnel rushed to his side. They lifted Jablonski onto a stretcher and carried him off the ice.

Jablonski was sent to an emergency room. Doctors soon brought the family bad news. Jablonski had been paralyzed from the elbows down. He would probably never walk again.

Catastrophic injuries such as this one are rare. However, they can be devastating. Situations like Jablonski's have fueled a debate about physical play in youth and high school sports. Sports such as ice hockey, football, and lacrosse naturally involve collisions. Some of the hits are unavoidable. However, there is a movement to cut down on the overall collisions in these sports. Doctors note that this is especially important in youth sports when kids aren't fully developed yet.

RULE CHANGES

Studies have shown that young athletes suffer more injuries the more they play. These athletes also suffer more injuries while playing more violent sports such as football. Injuries can range from minor muscle pulls to broken bones to catastrophic injuries, such as paralysis.

Coaches and league administrators have reacted to prevent these injuries. Youth football coaches monitor equipment for safety. They also strive to teach proper tackling techniques to players. Many head and shoulder injuries occur when players improperly try to tackle an opponent. In addition, many coaches have changed their approach to practice. Aggressive tackling drills are less common than they once were.

Lacrosse is one of the fastest growing sports in the United States. In 2011, US Lacrosse issued sweeping rule changes to youth lacrosse in the country. In boys' play, all goalies were required to wear arm pads and a protective cup. Hits on players in defenseless positions were banned. All body checking was banned at the Under-11 and Under-9 age groups. Only modified checking was permitted at the girls' Under-13 level. Younger girls are not allowed to check.

Organizations that govern youth hockey leagues have also adopted new rules. USA Hockey banned checking for kids 12 and under before the 2011–12 season. It also outlawed all blows to the head. Hockey Canada in spring 2013 also banned checking for players under 13. The organization governs youth leagues in that country.

NOT ALL ON BOARD

These decisions have generated controversy. Some coaches and parents argue that violence should not be modified in collision sports. These

▲ Peewee hockey players in Minnesota watch a game. All youth players in Minnesota must wear a "STOP" patch on their jerseys.

sports have always been physical, they argue. Changing the rules too much could fundamentally change the games. They also cite the need to teach kids the proper way to play physically at young ages. Older athletes in these sports still need to know how to check or tackle. So, despite evidence that says otherwise, some people worry that kids will be ill prepared once they reach those levels.

"They're learning the skill while they're learning other skills," the leader of one Canadian hockey association said. "They gain a lot more confidence when they're smaller. We feel they can get into some bad habits [if checking is not taught at a younger age]."

Many people also view sports as a learning tool for young people. They believe the physicality in sports helps kids develop mental toughness.

TRENDING TOWARD SAFETY

Regardless of these arguments, youth leagues continue to curb physical play.

Minnesota Hockey governs approximately 45,000 youth hockey players in that state. It approved rule changes just weeks after Jack Jablonski was paralyzed. Usually leagues adopt rule changes between seasons. Minnesota Hockey made an exception. The changes were agreed upon and enforced mid-season. Some of the rule changes toughened penalties for checking from behind and boarding. Referees now give a 5-minute major penalty or a 10-minute player misconduct for those violations.

"Retaining the tougher rules will not make youth hockey injury-free. Players may still get hurt, as they do in most every other sport," a Minneapolis *Star Tribune* editorial

"STOP"

Youth hockey players in Minnesota aren't old enough to drive. If they come up to an opponent from behind, however, they will see a stop sign. Minnesota Hockey ordered players to wear jerseys with a "STOP" patch stitched on their backs. It is meant to remind players coming from behind not to make an illegal or dangerous hit.

"I think it's important that we stress how dangerous the game of hockey is and that player safety has to come first," said Eric Olson, Minnesota Hockey's officiating director. "If this will help kids learn it and build a culture of not allowing checks from behind anywhere on the ice, then I think we're going to be successful."

Minnesota is a state that loves hockey. Naturally the rule changes to limit checking at young levels caused some controversy. The *Star Tribune* newspaper argued in favor of the checking ban in an editorial:

> *An increasing number of parents rightly worry about the growing body of conclusive medical evidence on the long-term impact of injuries—especially concussions. If those concerns go unaddressed by sports such as football and hockey, fewer parents are going to let their kids participate.*
>
> *Rule changes are only part of the solution. The attitudes of players, coaches, referees, and parents toward reducing or eliminating dangerous and illegal contact is critical as well.*
>
> *Fan behavior is a factor, too. Riding the refs for calling penalties and celebrating dangerous hits over finesse and speed can sometimes send the wrong message. And, no, we're not advocating banning legal contact.*
>
> Source: "Editorial: Minnesota Hockey minds 'STOP' sign." Star Tribune. Star Tribune, 29 June 2012. Web. 19 July 2013.

What's the Big Idea?

What point are the *Star Tribune* editorial writers trying to make in this piece? Is it an effective argument? How do you think somebody who disagrees with this opinion would respond? Put yourself in that person's shoes and write a few paragraphs to support the opposing opinion.

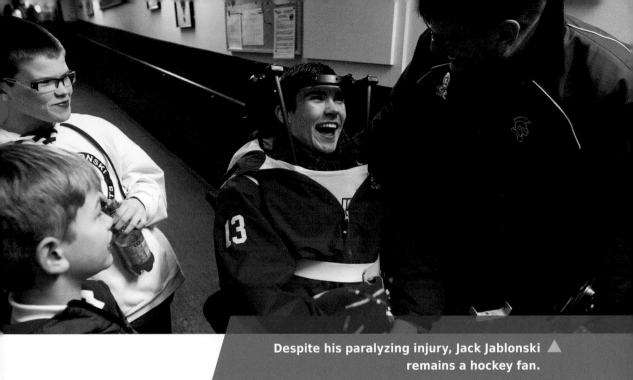

argued. "But the rules send a strong signal that checking from behind, boarding, and other illegal hits are dangerous and will not be tolerated."

People will continue to disagree with these limits on physical play. Catastrophic injuries such as the one suffered by Jablonski are very rare and largely preventable. Even Jablonski still favors checking in youth hockey. "The injury I had, it was a freak accident," he said. "You can't be soft, or totally take away hitting, because that's not hockey."

That is the challenge going forward. Hitting and physical play are important parts of these sports. Without those elements, the sports might fundamentally change. But the more physical the sport is, the more likely it is players could get injured.

CHAPTER 5

Minnesota Vikings running back Adrian Peterson is ▶
helped off the field after tearing his ACL during a 2011
game against the Washington Redskins.

MEDICAL ADVANCES

The December 2011 NFL game between the Minnesota Vikings and the Washington Redskins was relatively unimportant. Both teams were out of the running for the playoffs. The teams were just trying to end their seasons on a high note to prepare for the next season. But Vikings running back Adrian Peterson did not look at the game that way. He always plays as hard as he can. That is what made him the best running back of his generation.

However, it cost Peterson against the Redskins. He planted his leg on the ground just as a Redskins defender hit him. The impact tore Peterson's ACL.

Peterson was in agony as he had to be helped off the field. He was hurting both physically and emotionally. The injury felt awful. But Peterson was just as concerned about his career as the pain.

"I felt three pops and I knew it was my ACL," he said. "I remember saying to myself, 'Why me?'"

A torn ACL used to be a career-threatening injury for NFL players. That was especially true for running backs. Recovery typically took at least one full year. However, many players never fully recovered. The ACL helps players make cuts from side to side. Upon returning from a torn ACL, many players found their quickness and agility was never the same.

Advances in modern medicine have made this injury less devastating. A torn ACL can still limit a player's effectiveness forever. But as Peterson showed, it doesn't have to. Peterson underwent surgery. Then he worked tirelessly so he could play on opening day in September 2012. Over 16 games that season, Peterson rushed for 2,097 yards. Only one player in NFL history had rushed for more. Peterson was named the NFL Most Valuable Player (MVP) for his efforts.

"The tunnels of the knee joint are so well understood," according to *Sports Illustrated*, "that a modern ACL repair now nearly restores the [natural] architecture of the joint."

FASTER RECOVERIES

Peterson's recovery was extraordinary. He fully recovered faster than perhaps any other athlete with that injury. However, his recovery was part

A medical student and a physical therapist ▲
watch noted orthopedic surgeon James Andrews
perform surgery.

of a trend. Sports have become a big business in recent years. People invest a lot of money into teams and athletes. This is especially true on the professional level. Sports medicine has advanced greatly to help keep those athletes healthy. Some injuries that used to sideline players for a year or more are now much less devastating. This is due in part to better doctors and medical procedures. In addition, physical therapists and athletic trainers help an athlete rehabilitate.

"Athletic injuries are managed more successfully now than two or three decades ago," according to the *Journal of the American Academy of Orthopaedic Surgeons*.

There are now primary care sports medicine doctors. Orthopedic surgeons are often affiliated with sports medicine as well. Orthopedic medicine deals with bones and related issues. One of the biggest advances has been in arthroscopy. This is a type of surgery that involves a very small incision. Surgeons then use an instrument called an arthroscope to view the interior of a joint. In some cases, surgeons are even able to repair damage by using very small tools in other small incisions. The smaller incisions make for a much faster recovery than traditional surgery.

"Evolution in arthroscopy allows more accurate assessment of hip, ankle, shoulder, elbow, and wrist [injury], and possibly more successful management," according to a medical journal. "Increasingly, successful management of sports-related injuries has allowed more athletes to return to participation."

SIGNS OF IMPROVEMENT

Sports medicine has come a long way in only a few decades. Cincinnati Bengals quarterback Greg Cook injured his shoulder in the third game of the 1969 NFL season. Doctors did not even diagnose the injury to his throwing shoulder.

"I tore my rotator cuff and we didn't know it at the time because we didn't have the medical attention that you have today," Cook said. Nowadays, such a diagnosis is simple and rarely missed by doctors.

Cook returned to the lineup and continued playing that season. Doctors finally diagnosed the injury after the season. Then they spent three years trying to fix it. Cook's shoulder never properly healed.

He played only 12 games in his career. Just one of those games came after the 1969 season.

"The relatively primitive surgical procedure used for such injuries in the 1960s required cutting through muscles," according to NBC Sports, "which only [affected] Cook's shoulder further."

In the late 1970s, Bert Jones was one of the NFL's top quarterbacks. Then he too suffered an injury to his throwing shoulder. Jones had led the Baltimore Colts to three straight division titles. However, he missed much of the 1978 and 1979 seasons due to injury. He never regained his top form. Then, in 1982, he suffered a non-paralyzing broken neck that ended his career.

Jones and Cook essentially lost their careers to shoulder injuries that could be treated now. NFL quarterbacks still suffer shoulder injuries and running backs still suffer knee and ankle injuries. The big difference is that many of these injuries are now seen as temporary rather than career threatening. And today's players expect to eventually return to top form.

Drew Brees is one of the most prolific passers in NFL history. He suffered the same shoulder injury in the final game of the 2005 NFL season that Cook had suffered in 1969. Brees underwent successful surgery. He then rehabilitated the injury and returned the following season. It began only eight months after he suffered his injury. But Brees was healthy. And he promptly led his new team, the New Orleans Saints, to the conference championship game. From 2006 through 2012, Brees played in all but one game for the Saints.

TOMMY JOHN SURGERY

Top major league pitchers can throw the ball as fast as 100 miles per hour (161 km/h). However, throwing a baseball that fast causes great strain to the body. As such, pitchers often suffer shoulder and elbow injuries.

////////////////////////

ERIK KARLSSON

Erik Karlsson was named the NHL's top defenseman in 2011-12. However, in February 2013, the Ottawa Senators' star suffered a torn Achilles tendon. That is an injury that usually takes four to six months to recover from. Instead, he returned at the end of the regular season, just 10 weeks after suffering the injury. Karlsson's coach credited his quick return to "good genetics, work ethic [with his rehab], youth [he was 22], and the quality of [physical therapy] treatment." Karlsson's tendon had also not been completely severed.

Karlsson played in Ottawa's final three regular season games and all 10 postseason games. He tallied a goal and 11 assists, logging at least 25 minutes of ice time in 11 of 13 games.

////////////////

One of the most common injuries in baseball is a torn ulnar collateral ligament (UCL) in the elbow. The repetitive, violent throwing motion can cause this injury. However, a torn UCL can also come from just one bad throw.

In 1974, Los Angeles Dodgers left-hander Tommy John suffered this injury. He feared he would have to retire. His chances of ever pitching in MLB again were given as 1 in 100. However, a physician named Frank Jobe had an idea. He believed he could fix the injury by replacing the UCL with a tendon from elsewhere in John's body.

John underwent surgery later that year. He spent 18 months working to recover. Finally, in 1976, he pitched again for the

Dodgers. In fact, John continued pitching 14 more seasons until 1989. And he might have been better after the surgery. He won 164 games after his return. In 1977 and 1979, he finished second in voting for the National League (NL) Cy Young Award as the league's best pitcher.

"Tommy John surgery," as it became known, is now a common procedure among baseball players. Several major leaguers undergo the surgery each season. Most return to the majors in about one year. And many eventually find they can throw harder post-surgery. Among the pitchers who have successfully undergone Tommy John surgery are Chris Carpenter, John Smoltz, and Stephen Strasburg.

ALWAYS RISKS

Sports medicine is constantly improving. However, some injuries simply cannot be overcome. In 2010, Rutgers University defensive tackle Eric LeGrand collided with an opponent during a kickoff. The play caused an injury to LeGrand's spinal cord and left him paralyzed from the neck down. His football career was over in an instant. However, LeGrand has worked hard in physical therapy. Doctors initially gave him long odds of ever regaining body function. Yet he has regained some movement and someday hopes to walk again. "I'm going to keep fighting," LeGrand said. "I don't know when it's going to happen, but I know it is going to happen."

///////////////

RISK FACTORS

However, the surgery is not perfect. Chicago Cubs pitcher Kerry Wood took the baseball world by storm in 1998. The flame-throwing right-hander struck out 20 batters in one game. He was named the NL Rookie of the Year. Then he needed Tommy John surgery. Wood missed the entire 1999 season. He eventually became a solid major league pitcher. However, he never lived up to the hype from his rookie season.

Surgery can save an athlete's career. However, any surgery comes with great risks. Any time somebody's body is cut open, there is a chance for complications. That is what happened to Grant Hill. He had been a basketball star at Duke University and later for the Detroit Pistons. But he suffered a staph infection while undergoing ankle surgery in 2003. A staph infection is caused by certain bacteria entering deep into the body, often in the bloodstream, during surgery. Hill needed treatment for six months after the surgery just to regain his health.

As Hill learned, surgery is always risky. Despite the best treatment, sometimes things don't always get fixed or heal perfectly. New York

Grant Hill's promising professional basketball ▲
career was hampered by chronic injuries.

Yankees team doctor Chris Ahmad performed shoulder surgery on pitcher
Michael Pineda in 2012. But the best Ahmad could predict was that he
was "cautiously optimistic" that Pineda would fully recover. Like many
procedures, "shoulder surgery is challenging," Ahmad said.

In addition, surgery cannot treat every injury. In fact, the vast majority
of sports injuries do not require surgery. Sometimes athletes simply must
rest, rehab, and allow injuries to heal. Pulled ligaments and stiff, inflamed
muscles are examples of such injuries.

CHAPTER 6

Quarterback Brett Favre played through several injuries during his career. He started a record 297 consecutive NFL games from 1992 to 2010. ▶

HOW TO HANDLE INJURY

I n 1925, New York Yankees first baseman Wally Pipp sat out a game because he was not feeling well. Pipp was replaced in the lineup by 22-year-old Lou Gehrig. Gehrig famously played in the next 2,130 consecutive games for the Yankees. Gehrig likely would have taken over as the starter eventually. But because Pipp sat out, he lost his starting job that day. The Yankees traded him after the season. New York went on to win multiple championships over the next decade. Meanwhile, Pipp floundered with the Cincinnati Reds.

Nearly a century later, the legend of Wally Pipp still serves as a warning. Dozens of athletes have lost their starting roles because they

sat out with injury. This fear of losing a starting role while injured causes many athletes to play hurt or rush through the recovery process. Their status with the team is just one of many factors athletes must consider in deciding when to return from injury.

PLAYING THROUGH PAIN

Athletes play through injury for a number of reasons. They might fear losing their starting role with the team. They might be eager to prove their toughness to teammates, management, and fans. Or maybe their team is on a roll, and they don't want to risk letting their teammates down.

The modern NFL is littered with players who lost their jobs due to injury. Jeremy Shockey was celebrated for being an iron man. The tight end started 59 of 62 games for the New York Giants between 2004 and 2007. He had earned Pro Bowl selections four times in his six-year career. Plus he had the fourth-most catches of any player in Giants history.

But Shockey broke his leg late in the 2007 season. Rookie Kevin Boss replaced Shockey in the starting lineup. The Giants then won four playoff games without Shockey, including the Super Bowl. So the team traded Shockey during the offseason and made Boss the full-time starter. Shockey and the team had other issues as well. But the injury was the turning point in Shockey losing the starting role.

Sometimes athletes play through injuries to demonstrate toughness. Male pro sports leagues are characterized by a macho culture. Players must constantly prove they are manly enough to handle the grind.

Laveranues Coles dislocated his middle finger during an NFL game in the 2004 season. The Washington Redskins' wide receiver jogged to the sidelines, popped his finger back into place, and returned to the game.

"When we all step on the field, it should be all out," Coles said after the game. "You're man enough to be out there; you're man enough to accept the consequences. That's the way I play the game, and that's the way I feel everybody should play it."

TAKING THEIR TIME

There is tremendous pressure on professional athletes to quickly return from injuries. However, some athletes have led the way by putting their own health above the team's success.

Chicago Bulls point guard Derrick Rose was the National Basketball Association (NBA) MVP in 2010–11. However, he suffered an ACL injury during the 2012 playoffs. Rose missed the entire 2012–13 regular season. Doctors cleared Rose to play late in the season, but he continued to sit out.

The media, fans, and even other NBA players criticized Rose. They thought if

INJURIES FROM HEAD TO TOE

Perhaps no athlete faces more pressure to play through injury than one taking part in the Stanley Cup playoffs. NHL players rarely miss a playoff game unless the injury is so severe that he would hurt the team by playing. In 2009, the Washington Capitals fielded a team with injuries from shoulders to feet during the playoffs. Defenseman Mike Green played with an injured shoulder, winger Alex Semin an injured thumb, and defenseman Tom Poti had a broken foot. Winger Alex Ovechkin took painkillers before every game. NHL teams attempt to protect their injured players by offering little to no information about their injuries to the press. Reports say players have "upper body" or "lower body" injuries instead of, say, a dislocated shoulder or charley horse. Teams don't want to give opponents a clue about where their players are ailing.

Chicago Bulls point guard Derrick Rose works out before a game in February 2013. Rose sat out the entire 2012-13 season with a knee injury.

doctors had cleared him and the Bulls needed him, he should be playing. But Rose never felt comfortable on his knee during practice. He worried about reinjuring it. So he missed the entire postseason.

Chicago fans were also hard on Bears quarterback Jay Cutler. He was knocked out of an NFL conference championship game against the Green Bay Packers in January 2011. Cutler briefly returned to the game. But he could not plant his foot and throw. So Cutler left the game for good in the third quarter. He had to sit and watch the Bears' backup quarterbacks fail to lead a comeback.

The TV cameras often showed Cutler watching from the sidelines. From afar, he didn't appear to be obviously injured. So fans, the media, and other NFL players ripped into him. They said it was his duty to play through the pain because he gave his team the best chance to win. It was only after the game that the diagnosis came out. Cutler had sprained the medial collateral ligament (MCL) in his knee. That would have made it nearly impossible for him to play with any effectiveness.

Still, incidents like those put player safety in the spotlight. Players such as Rose and Cutler faced great pressure, but they took a stand that their health was more important than winning. Not all fans and media members could understand why the athletes thought that way. But many players defended the decision to sit out.

"Jay was hurt, obviously," teammate Brian Urlacher said. "There's no reason for him to be out there if he can't get it done. He was obviously hurt pretty bad or he would have played . . . For them to question his toughness is stupid to me."

MIXED RESULTS

Sometimes athletes who play through injuries become legends. New York Knicks center Willis Reed tore a muscle in his leg during the 1970 NBA Finals. But he hobbled onto the court and helped his team beat the Los Angeles Lakers in Game 7.

"I wanted to play," he said. "That was the championship, the one great moment we had all played for since 1969. I didn't want to have to look at myself in the mirror 20 years later and say that I wished I had tried to play."

Reed eventually recovered enough to play four more NBA seasons. He even helped the Knicks win another championship in 1973.

Grant Hill was not as fortunate. Hill rushed back from an ankle injury to play in the 2000 NBA postseason for the Detroit Pistons. Detroit lost in the first round and the star forward reinjured his ankle. The joint never fully recovered. Hill later underwent multiple surgeries throughout his career. He never returned to an All-Star level. Hill blamed that partly on his injuries being mismanaged by his teams and their doctors.

STAYING SAFE

Athletes, coaches, trainers, and doctors can try to minimize the risk for injuries in sports. But as long as there is physical activity, injuries can never fully be eliminated.

Sports leagues are constantly working to make their games safer. This might be done through better equipment, tweaked rules, or better awareness of risks. However, football will always involve players crashing

BLOODY SOCK

In 2004, Boston Red Sox pitcher Curt Schilling underwent emergency surgery to tie a loose tendon in his right ankle. Normally this would cause a player to take time off to rest and recover. But the surgery took place during the MLB playoffs. Schilling's ankle had not fully healed. He risked severe long-term damage if he pitched. But he did anyway. Schilling took the mound and helped his team beat the rival New York Yankees 4–2 in Game 6. He allowed just four hits and one run in seven innings. He continued to pitch even as a suture used in his surgery came undone and his ankle started to bleed. The Red Sox went on to win their first World Series since 1918 that season.

into each other at high speeds. Baseball will always have pitchers who violently whip their arms to throw the ball. Even sports such as running or golf will always involve physical exertion that can lead to muscle strains, overuse injuries, or freak accidents.

If a player is injured, he or she now has more and better options for recovery. With advances in sports medicine, injuries that once threatened careers can now be repaired in a matter of months. Skilled surgeons and athletic trainers can help an injured athlete get back to full strength.

However, it is important to remember that all sports have risks. Some injuries cannot be repaired or lead to lifetime effects. That is why it is important to follow the rules when playing and to check with a doctor or trainer to help with any injury.

TERRELL DAVIS

Adrian Peterson's triumph in 2012 came only a decade after Terrell Davis had failed in his quest to overcome a similar serious knee injury. Davis had been the NFL's top running back from 1995 to 1998. He rushed for 6,413 yards and 56 rushing touchdowns during that time with the Denver Broncos. However, Davis tore both his ACL and MCL early in the 1999 season. He never came close to regaining his top form. Davis came back in 2000. Despite still being in his 20s, he rushed for 983 yards and just two touchdowns over 13 games in 2000 and 2001. Then he retired. Those types of declines were the norm for years with ACL injuries.

"What Peterson has shown this season is that it's possible—through a combination of hard work, self-confidence, and an otherworldly genetic makeup—to come back stronger," a *New York Times* article said.

One thing coaches often say is that players should not focus on injuries while playing. They say a player who is distracted and thinking about getting injured is more likely to get injured. That is a mantra that many athletes follow.

Changing the rules will only go so far to counter overly physical play and prevent injury. Many people believe a change within sporting culture is necessary. They prefer to celebrate skill and team play over physical play. Professional lacrosse player Brodie Merrill noted that he favored reform of his sport to improve player safety. He wrote:

> *I think we need to take a serious look at the role of contact in our sport. Do the big hits make the game what it is? I don't think so and I don't think we would miss them if they were gone.*

> Source: Merrill, Brodie. "Wingin' It: My Concussion, and Rethinking the Role of Contact in Contact Sports." philly.com. Interstate General Media LLC. *13 March 2013. Web. 19 July 2013.*

On the other side of the argument was the father of a 10-year-old youth football player. He told *Sports Illustrated*:

> *I want my son to learn the fundamentals. But I also want him to play it as a tough, physical game, because that's what separates it from most other sports.*

> Source: Farrell Evans. "Early Warning: Even at the Pee Wee Level, Coaches Struggle to Balance Safety Concerns with Teaching Toughness." SI Vault. *Time Inc., Nov. 2010. Web. 19 July 2013.*

What's the Big Idea?

People share many different views about physicality in sports. Which side are you on? Write a few paragraphs explaining whether or not you think the NHL should allow fighting and back your stance up with evidence from the book.

A trainer treats Colorado Rockies batter Carlos ▲
Gonzalez after Gonzalez was struck by a foul ball
during a 2013 game.

"I don't let injuries scare me," former New York Jets quarterback Chad
Pennington said. "Injuries are part of this game. If you play scared, if you
play not to get injured, you get injured."

DISCUSSION QUESTIONS

Another View

Do you agree with the recent decisions by youth hockey and lacrosse organizations to restrain physical play? Why or why not? Read as many articles as you can find about the new rules adopted by US Lacrosse, Hockey Canada, and Minnesota Hockey. Think about the points of view expressed by people who oppose these rules. Do you agree with them?

You Are There

Imagine you suffer an injury while playing sports. Your team's season is not over and your injury is not too severe. In fact, a doctor says you could play with the injury, but it's possible you might worsen the injury by playing. Would you play with the injury? Why or why not?

Take a Stand

Do you think Robert Griffin III should have removed himself from the playoff game against the Seattle Seahawks? What about his coach? Should he have removed Griffin at any point? Why or why not? Take a side in this debate. Write a short essay arguing your side.

Dig Deeper

Which do you think is the most pressing issue within the world of sports injuries today? How come? What do you think might happen if this issue is not addressed soon? Ask an adult to help you research sports injuries. Read a few articles and write a short blog post about this issue.

anti-inflammatory pills

Medication designed to reduce pain and swelling in the body.

arthroscopy

An operation to repair a damaged joint, in which the surgeon uses an instrument called an arthroscope to examine the interior of the joint.

cortisone shots

Injections designed to relieve pain and swelling in a certain area of the body in the short term.

degenerative

When an organ loses function due to deteriorating tissue.

ligament

Connective tissue in the body that connects two bones or holds together a joint.

orthopedics

The branch of medicine that treats the musculoskeletal system, which includes bones, joints, and muscles.

reconstructive surgery

An operation conducted to rebuild a damaged or lost structure within the body.

sprain

When a ligament is stretched too far or tears, it causes a sprain. The joint swells and becomes painful.

strain

When a muscle becomes overstretched and tears, it has been strained. Also called a pulled muscle, strains can be very painful.

tendon

Tissue in the body that attaches a muscle to a bone.

FOR MORE INFORMATION

SELECTED BIBLIOGRAPHY

Jenkins, Sally, and Rick Maese and Scott Clement. "Do No Harm: Retired NFL Players Endure a Lifetime of Hurt." *The Washington Post*. The Washington Post, 16 May 2013. Web. 8 Aug. 2013.

Maske, Mark. *War Without Death: A Year of Extreme Competition in Pro Football's NFC East*. New York: Penguin, 2007. Print.

Schneider, Karen S. "The Way We Play the Game." *SI Vault*. Time Inc., 27 Feb. 2012. Web. 8 Aug. 2013.

Sowell, Mike. *One Pitch Away: The Players' Stories of the 1986 League Championships and World Series*. New York: Macmillan, 1995. Print.

FURTHER READINGS

Andrews, James R., and Don Yaeger. *Any Given Monday: Sports Injuries and How to Prevent Them for Athletes, Parents, and Coaches—Based on My Life in Sports Medicine*. New York: Scribner, 2013. Print.

Barber, Tiki, and Gil Reavill. *Tiki: My Life in the Game and Beyond*. New York: Simon Spotlight Entertainment, 2007. Print.

Feinstein, John. *Next Man Up: A Year Behind the Lines in Today's NFL*. New York: Back Bay, 2007. Print.

Walker, Brad. *The Anatomy of Sports Injuries*. Berkeley, CA: North Atlantic, 2007. Print.

WEB SITES

To learn more about injuries in sports, visit ABDO Publishing Company online at **www.abdopublishing.com**. Web sites about injuries in sports are featured on our Book Links page. These links are routinely monitored and updated to provide the most current information available.

PLACES TO VISIT

Carnegie Science Center's Highmark SportsWorks
1 Allegheny Avenue
Pittsburgh, PA 15212
412-237-3400
www.carnegiesciencecenter.org/exhibits/highmark-sportsworks
This center, which is part of the Carnegie Science Center, aims "to inspire learning and curiosity by uniting the experience of sports for every age level with the laws of science that control sports." The nearly 30 interactive experiences are in three areas: LifeWorks, Physics of Sports, and Sports Challenge.

International Museum of Surgical Science
1524 North Lake Shore Drive
Chicago, IL 60610
312-642-6502
www.imss.org/index.htm
This museum offers exhibits about developments in surgery throughout history, focusing on science, health, and culture. The collections include art and artifacts.

INDEX

ABOUT THE AUTHOR

Ryan Basen is a researcher and former journalist with the *Charlotte Observer* who now lives in the Washington DC area. He won the NC Press Association Sports News Reporting award in 2008. He also earned Honorable Mention Investigative Reporting honors from the Associated Press Sports Editors in 2007. Ryan has also written for the *New York Times, Washington Post, Baltimore Sun,* Associated Press, and *Charlotte* magazine. He has written several books as well, including biographies of professional athletes and histories of pro teams.